KOBUS BOTHA

Photography
JAN HENDRIK
VAN DER WESTHUIZEN

Translation by
NICOLE SEEMAN

Le Braai

Braai with a bit of *je ne sais quoi*

CONTENTS

Introduction 9

Braai equipment 12

Preparing the fire 14

Choosing the ingredients and the cooking method 16

Taking care of your braai 18

Cooking on a stick 23

Meat and poultry 41

Fish and seafood 81

Sides, vegetables, fruits and breads 99

Salads and rubs 127

Index 140

INTRODUCTION

🔥 **When I think of the past, in my happiest memories, there is always fire and a braai.**

I grew up in the Klein Karoo, on a farm, where we braaied several times a week. They were always good times, festive and joyful. We also went to the sea, which was 60 kilometres away, behind a mountain; there we would fish and then braai what we had caught. Few things are as nice as sitting outside, smelling grilled food, and watching the flames of a fire.

My journey, which started on a farm in the Karoo, in a house without running water or electricity, where you had to walk 50 metres outside to go to the toilet, has taken quite a few turns. I went to nine different schools, two universities, before taking up a career as a film producer that took me all over the world.

I love conjuring up my fondest food memories in my adopted country, especially in a city like Paris, where any cooking with fire has largely been forgotten.

> Today, one of my greatest pleasures is to light a fire in the heart of Paris and braai for thousands of people.

Few things bring me as much pleasure as watching people enjoy the food I cook on the barbecue, near the Seine, surrounded by history and culture. The French took me in with open arms. My barbecue activities have really developed over the past few years and I'm also very lucky that the press love my barbecues, or maybe it's just my beard.

I teach many barbecue classes. I enjoy doing it as there are never more than twenty 'students' at a time. I can show them how to cook many lovely things, like the ones I'm sharing with you here. As an added bonus, they have to listen to all my stories...

🔥 **A braai isn't just about food**

Some of my best memories of braais are about fishing with my father on the wild coasts of South Africa. We would walk for half a day, camp by the sea, fish with a rod or a spear gun. As there were many fish, we were sure we'd be successful, so we started the fire when we got there. As soon as we caught our first fish, the fire was ready. We'd be together, facing an angry sea, with a fire, and the lovely smell of super-fresh fish on the grill. To this day, I cannot imagine a better meal.

South Africans love to gather around a fire with family and friends, at home, in the bush, or at the beach. At night, if you lift your eyes, you can see the stars overhead, like in a planetarium. As the wood burns to coals, we tell tales and share stories.

When you make a braai in South Africa, the guests arrive help to prepare the fire and cook the food. Everyone pitches in, giving their opinion about the equipment, the cooking method, the ingredients… I love the way the French talk about food when they're eating: they share memories, recipes, addresses. In South Africa, these conversations take place when the braai is being prepared. It's not just about eating. You share a lot more than food with your family and friends.

🔥 Braaiing is the jazz of cooking

I often make this comparison because, as in jazz, with a braai you can improvise. And the better you can 'play' the richer and more interesting your improvisations will become. Of course, with cooking, as with music, you have to master the basic melody, and then you can – and I encourage you to do it – add your personal touch.

A braai is about feeling. You need to use all your senses to know if food is cooked, if the seasoning is good, how to combine ingredients… Sight, smell, touch, of course taste, and even hearing, will be your 'kitchen instruments' to play wonderful delicious music that will delight your audience.

I wrote this book to introduce what I call the 'jazz of cooking' to as many people as possible. I want everyone to discover this pleasure and to demonstrate that anyone can make a very good braai. I chose to make the book not too big, so that it's easy to take everywhere: on holidays, for a weekend away…

I love to introduce people to braaiing, to show them all the different foods they can cook, the many ingredients, including some that I've discovered here in France. Here there are wonderful products, but people don't always think to cook them on a braai. I hope I have convinced you to try your hand at it and to make your own 'jazz'.

Well, enjoy the book! You can track my fires all over France and stay in contact, if you wish. What I do and where I go on Facebook @kobusbraai, lusty pics of braai food on Instagram @kobusbraai, website with photographs of all my events, press clippings etc., www.kobusbraai.fr and videos on the YouTube channel **Kobus Braai**.

Happy braaiing!
KOBUS BOTHA

> A braai is about feeling; you have to use all your senses.

As in jazz, with braai you can improvise.

BRAAI EQUIPMENT

There are many ways to make a braai, but the simplest is an open fire, on the ground, surrounded by stones on which to rest a grid. I own a number of different types of braai, including a massive barrel-shaped one that I use for catering, which weighs over three tons, but I still prefer cooking with an open fire. Sitting around a fire watching food cook is one of life's greater pleasures.

🔥 The braai

All the recipes in this book can be prepared on any braai with direct heat (which means that the food cooks on a grid placed directly over the heat source). Ideally, you should have enough space to allow for the grid and a fire on the side, so you can make new coals while you're cooking, as the coals will be too hot at first and, in general, they don't last long enough if you're cooking a large meal. If you can have a live fire producing coals as well as control over the height of your grid, you're in the braai equivalent of a perfect kitchen.

> Part of the pleasure comes from the fire itself. It's in our genes: watching a fire makes us happy!

🔥 Tools and accessories

I use a minimum of equipment, because I believe that you can prepare a lot of things with very few tools, and I've written this book with that in mind. (But, if you're like me, and you love kitchen gadgets, there's nothing to stop you going wild and buying lots of specialised accessories!) My essential tools include:

→ **Tongs** You need these to turn ingredients easily and move them around the grid; they should be comfortable to hold, close easily, be easy to clean, and quite long. Have a second set of tongs for moving hot coals.

→ **Hinged grid** I use this to hold delicate ingredients, like fish, or for when I'll need to turn several similar-sized pieces of meat at the same time.

→ **Basting brush** Choose a wide one for brushing on marinades or sauces while the meat is cooking. If you're away from home and don't have a brush, try rolled-up lettuce or spinach leaves (it works, I promise you!).

→ **Wire brush** You need a stiff-bristled brush to clean the grid before you start cooking.

→ **Small frying pan or saucepan** Cast iron is perfect, or choose an old pan that you're not too attached to as it'll get very black. Place it directly on the braai to melt butter or keep sauces and marinades warm.

→ **Grill pan with small holes** Ideal for cooking sliced vegetables or smaller pieces of chicken and meat.

→ **Basic cooking tools** To avoid having to run back and forwards to the kitchen, gather everything you need beforehand, such as separate chopping boards for raw and cooked meat, chef's knife or carving knife, long-handled fork, metal spatula for turning food, metal or bamboo skewers (sosatie sticks), platters or roasting pans for holding cooked meat, heavyweight foil to protect tender foods or keep cooked items warm, braai gloves (mitts) or a clean kitchen cloth for handling hot dishes, etc.

Wood, charcoal or gas?

Wood, charcoal, briquettes or gas ? Each has its pros and cons:

→ Gas is perfect when there's no time to prepare coals, because it heats very quickly and gives food a nicer taste than cooking in a pan. When you don't have a lot of time, but you really fancy a braai, gas is your friend.

→ Charcoal makes good, hot coals, but they burn out quite quickly. Choose large chunks, as they'll last a little longer. Charcoal is best for an open braai, so you can continue to add hot coals while you cook. Most food cooks well on charcoal.

→ **Briquettes** can give food an unpleasant smell and taste if you don't prepare them properly; they should be ashy and grey before you start cooking. Their advantage is that they stay hot longer than charcoal, making them ideal for kettle braais. If you need to add more briquettes, use a separate fire starter (chimney starter) to heat them up. Buy good quality briquettes made from hardwood; they're more expensive but they're worth it.

→ Wood and fire are synonymous. For me, part of the pleasure of braaiing comes from the fire itself; watching the flames always makes me happy. Most people let a wood fire burn entirely to coals, but I prefer to keep some extra wood going on the side, both for the atmosphere and to allow me to add more coals as I cook.

PREPARING *the fire*

When I was a kid, the challenge was to start a fire with just one match. It was a question of honour, so one had to succeed, even in the rain. When you grow up making fires outdoors, you get used to doing it safely, without scorching any nearby vegetation. If you only make the occasional braai fire, you need to learn how to do it properly.

The traditional way

The traditional way to start a fire is to choose something that burns easily, like pine cones or crumpled newspaper, for example. Next, add kindling (small pieces of wood) that will burn for longer and give a stronger flame. Once that is going, start to add whatever is going to burn the longest, like chunks of wood or lumps of charcoal. If you're using wood, make sure it's dry and untreated. For the fire to catch, you might have to fan it with a piece of cardboard to keep the flames going and build up a good blaze. As soon as you have a good layer of coals, you can start to braai.

The modern way

I have to confess that I use a high-pressure gas tool that can start a fire in a few seconds. It was made to order for me, so you won't find it in stores. As I barbecue for over a thousand people at a time, I can't afford to have things go wrong, and I often don't have much time. Otherwise I use a blowtorch. It's a clean and quick way to start a fire. You aim it at one part of the wood until it catches fire, then at another, and so on. I also use it to melt metal and make crème brûlée, making it a wise investment. But, if you have two left hands, using a blowtorch might incinerate you and your friends, so get a slow-burning refillable fire lighter.

If you use firelighters, choose those made with natural products, to reduce the smell of paraffin when you light the fire. Make sure that any chemical products have completely burnt down before starting to cook food.

🔥 How long does it take?

Wood 30–45 minutes from lighting to coals. Don't leave an open fire unattended.

Charcoal 10–15 minutes from lighting to coals. As soon as charcoal starts to burn and give off heat, you can start to cook your food.

Briquettes About 20 minutes until they turn ash-grey. Don't put uncovered food on the cooking grid until they are ready.

Gas Ready in about 5 minutes; this is the speediest method.

🔥 Managing the temperature of your braai

To lower the temperature of your braai (for delicate ingredients, or those that need long, slow cooking), you need to spread the coals thinly, or push some coals to one side so you have two cooking temperatures on the same braai. To increase the temperature, you need to pile up the coals under the food. If you want your braai to last, make a lot of coals, so you can move them around as necessary.

CHOOSING THE INGREDIENTS
and the cooking method

It goes without saying that you should choose quality ingredients. Braaiing is a cooking method that makes the most of simple ingredients. It is neither pretentious nor fancy (although you can braai pricey cuts of meat or luxury ingredients like salmon and crayfish).

When it comes to meat, thicker cuts tend to braai better than thin pieces, and chicken is best with the skin on. Likewise, vegetables and fish need a protective skin or peel to prevent them from burning or drying out. Wrap delicate ingredients, or those that you have cut into small pieces, in baking (greaseproof) paper and then in foil and seal the parcel well. If necessary, pat dry all foods before cooking, and season to taste with salt and pepper.

One always thinks of braaiing meat, but vegetarians can braai too; you'll find recipes for fruits and vegetables in this book.

What gives braaied food its special flavour?

Many braai fundis don't like cooking with gas because they say that food doesn't taste the same as when cooked over coals. While there might be some truth in this, what one misses most with a gas braai is the 'real' fire atmosphere. To tell the truth, wood and charcoal don't really give foods a smoky flavour. To get that, you need a smoker, where the heat comes from smouldering logs that are separate from the food, which is really cooked by the smoke. But whether you cook on wood or gas, everyone loves the irresistible smell of grilled meat; it just makes you want to eat.

The aroma of grilled meat comes from the cooking of the fat and the juices that run onto the braai and evaporate. (Put the cooking grid at least 10 cm above the coals to avoid carcinogenic products coming back onto the food.)

TAKING CARE
of your braai

🔥 To me, the best way to look after a braai is to do almost nothing. I don't clean the grid after cooking, I leave any food residue clinging to the grid, because the natural oils will stop it from rusting. The next time I use the braai, I put the grid directly in the fire, allowing the intense heat to burn off any food residue. Then I just need to brush the grid or wipe it with paper towels to clean it easily.

🔥 When the fire has cooled down, you should dispose of any ashes that are left in the base of a braai, as they attract humidity, which could lead to rust or create holes in a metal braai.

🔥 If you're cooking different foods on the same grid (meat and fish, for example), brush it with a wire brush or wipe it with paper towels between batches, to avoid ending up with some rather unusual flavours! Protect your hands, so you don't get burnt.

COOKING
ON A STICK

Curried CHICKEN SOSATIES

Sosaties are a great way to cook small pieces of meat left on a chicken carcass, so they don't go to waste. We would simply poke them onto a stick. Now it's become a way of cooking in itself. This recipe is always a success as the sauce makes the chicken really tasty.

SERVES 4

3–4 skinless, deboned chicken breasts

4 soft-dried apricots

4 pitted prunes

4 wooden or bamboo skewers, soaked in water beforehand

CURRY SAUCE

1 tablespoon sunflower or canola oil

12 pearl onions, peeled but left whole

1 tablespoon mild curry powder

1 tablespoon smooth apricot jam

1 tablespoon white vinegar

½ cup dry white wine

salt to taste

The day before

🔥 Heat the oil in a saucepan and sauté the onions until soft and lightly coloured.

🔥 Add the curry powder and stir.

🔥 Add the apricot jam, vinegar and wine and cook until the mixture turns syrupy. Leave to cool, then pour into a non-metallic dish.

🔥 Cut the chicken into bite-sized pieces. Season with salt.

🔥 Cut the apricots and prunes in half.

🔥 Add the chicken and fruit to the curry sauce and stir to coat.

🔥 Cover with cling wrap and marinate in the fridge overnight (or for at least 6 hours).

The same day

Keep 8 onions whole and cut the remaining 4 onions into pieces that you'll be able to thread onto the skewers.

Prepare the skewers by alternating pieces of chicken, apricots, prunes and onions. (Start and end with a whole onion.)

Place the sosaties on a cooking grid above the coals. The curry sauce burns quickly, so keep an eye on them and turn them often. Brush frequently with the leftover sauce.

Cook for approximately 12 minutes.

You can cook sausages at the same time as these skewers.

Sweet and sour LAMB KIDNEY AND LIVER SKEWERS

I created this recipe from a dish my mother used to make me for breakfast. But not everyone wants to eat kidneys and liver in the morning, so I decided to adapt this recipe for the braai. It's totally irresistible!

SERVES 4

4 lamb kidneys (with some fat from around the kidneys)

1 lamb's liver

salt and black pepper to taste

4 bamboo or wooden skewers, soaked in water beforehand

SWEET AND SOUR SAUCE

¾ cup water

2 tablespoons white vinegar

1 tablespoon castor sugar

1 tablespoon flour

1 tablespoon butter

- Cut the kidneys, liver and fat into bite-sized pieces.
- Thread the skewers, alternating the pieces of kidney and liver with small pieces of fat. Season with salt and pepper.
- Grill the skewers for about 12 minutes, turning them from time to time (not too often), so a crust forms on the meat. Drizzle with sauce before serving.
- To make the sauce, place a small flameproof saucepan on the grid over very hot coals. Pour in ¾ cup water and bring to a boil. Combine the vinegar, sugar and flour in a small bowl. Add the mixture to the boiling water, then add the butter and whisk until smooth. When it starts to thicken, set it aside. Serve with the kidney and liver skewers.

Place the skewers on a bed of boiled rice before drizzling them with the sauce.

'SKINLESS' *coriander sausages*

When I travel, I always like to taste what people are cooking over fire. I discovered this recipe in Morocco, where you can buy freshly cooked kebabs in the souks or from roadside stalls. Every seller has his own recipe, and they are all delicious. This is a great way to prepare sausages without too much fuss. Why not create your own version with the meats and spices you like.

SERVES 4–6

1 kg lamb mince (not lean mince)

1 bunch fresh coriander leaves

2 tablespoons coriander seeds, roughly crushed

2 teaspoons salt

1 teaspoon fine white pepper

4–6 skewers (flat metal skewers are traditional)

A few hours in advance

- Put the meat into a bowl and place it in the freezer for about 30 minutes.
- Chop the coriander leaves finely and add to the bowl with the meat. Add the seasonings and mix with your hands until the ingredients are well combined (work quickly, so the meat doesn't warm up). Taste, and adjust the seasoning if necessary.
- Divide the meat into 4–6 portions. Roll each one into a sausage shape and thread onto the skewers, pressing the meat firmly so it won't fall apart during cooking. Keep the skewers in the fridge until you are ready to cook them.

Cooking the skewers

Grill the skewers for 5–8 minutes per side, until they get a nice brown crust. (You'll need to hold the skewers in your hands over the flames, or place two bricks on the grid and rest the skewers on them. If you put the skewers directly onto the grid, the meat will stick to it.)

Serve with a salad or thinly shaved ribbons of raw butternut.

Peri peri PRAWNS

South Africans just love these spicy prawns, which have their origin in Mozambique.

SERVES 4

1 whole head garlic
1 lemon
4 tablespoons butter
200 ml dry white wine
2 teaspoons peri peri (or chilli) powder
½ teaspoon salt
20–24 whole medium prawns
4 bamboo or wooden skewers, soaked in water beforehand

- Cut the head of garlic in half through the cloves. Cut the lemon into thick slices. Place the garlic (cut side down) and the lemon slices on the braai and grill until lightly browned. Don't let the garlic burn.
- Place the butter in a small saucepan on the grid and allow it to melt. Add the braaied garlic and lemon slices, the wine, peri peri powder and salt and stir to combine. Cook until the sauce reduces and becomes syrupy. Adjust the seasoning if necessary.
- Using a sharp knife, split the prawns along the back and remove the black vein. Thread 5–6 prawns onto each skewer, piercing them through the head and tail, so they fit closely together.
- Place the skewers on the grid over hot coals. Brush with the sauce while they cook. Grill the prawns on one side until the shells are crispy. Turn them over and brush again with the sauce. When both sides are crispy, remove the skewers from the braai.
- Peel the prawns and eat them with your fingers, dipping them in the remaining sauce.

Serve with white rice, with some extra lemon wedges on the side.

Sweet and sour MUSHROOM SKEWERS

I got the inspiration for this recipe from the only Western American-style restaurant that there was in South Africa when I was young. They served delicious mushrooms just like these.

FOR 10 SKEWERS

- 40–60 large button mushrooms
- 10 bamboo or wooden skewers, soaked in water beforehand

SWEET AND SOUR SAUCE

- ½ cup soy sauce
- ¼ cup water
- 2 tablespoons sweet white wine
- 150 g brown sugar
- 1 tablespoon chopped garlic
- 1 tablespoon chopped fresh ginger

- Thread the mushrooms onto the skewers. Set aside while you prepare the sauce.
- Combine all the sauce ingredients in a small saucepan. Cook over a low heat until the sugar dissolves.
- Brush the mushrooms with the sauce.
- Position the barbecue grid about 15 cm above the coals (any lower, and the sauce could burn).
- Place the skewers on the grid. Turn them often to prevent them from burning. It's important to cook the mushrooms quickly, so the juices don't run out. They should be hot, but they don't have to be cooked right through. Keep brushing them with sauce as they cook.
- Slide the mushrooms off the skewers and serve.

Serve straight from the fire, otherwise the mushrooms will get soft.

STICK BREAD

Baguette on a braai! When I was a child, we often used to cook this bread on an open fire in the bush. We would hold the hot bread in one hand, and a pigeon or some other bird we were grilling in the other. We used acacia branches as skewers, which added a pleasant flavour and had thorns to hold the pigeon.

FOR 1 BREAD

bread dough (see page 116)
flour, for dusting

- Prepare the bread dough from the basic recipe (if you have too much, save the surplus in the fridge, wrapped in cling film).
- For each stick bread, make a ball of dough the size of a fist.
- Roll the dough into 20-cm-long sausages, about 2 cm wide.
- Use thick skewers or dowel sticks, or cut clean, dry sticks from your garden (if you are sure the tree is non-toxic); they should be about 30 cm long.
- Dust the sticks with flour. Twist each sausage around a stick, pinching the ends of the dough to help it stay in place. Place the sticks on the grid. Turn them often, until the bread is golden brown and crusty. When it is cooked, it should have a hollow sound if you knock on it.

You should eat this bread directly off the stick.

S'MORES

Kids and adults love these S'mores, which are very popular in the USA around a camp fire. The name comes from the fact that, once you've had one, you want 's'more' (some more). August 10th has even been declared National S'mores Day.

MAKES 1 S'MORE

FOR EACH S'MORE YOU'LL NEED:

2–3 marshmallows

2–3 squares of milk or dark chocolate (enough to cover the biscuit when melted)

2 plain biscuits (Tennis, Marie or tea biscuits)

1 bamboo or wooden skewer, soaked in water beforehand

🔥 The secret to a good S'more is how you cook the marshmallows. Thread them on a stick or skewer and turn them slowly over the flames until they are nicely caramelized (but not burnt) on the outside and runny in the centre. You have to be patient and not hold your stick too close to the fire.

🔥 When the marshmallows are ready, place them and the chocolate squares between the two biscuits and squeeze gently, allowing the heat of the marshmallows to melt the chocolate a little.
A real treat! (You can also melt the chocolate ahead of time and spread it on the biscuits.)

Variations

- Combine chocolate and peanut butter, or use just peanut butter.
- Use salted butter caramel instead of chocolate.
- Try chocolate chip cookies instead of plain biscuits.
- For French S'mores, toast pieces of baguette in place of biscuits.
- Jam S'mores, with strawberry jam instead of chocolate.
- Club S'mores, with layers of chocolate and marshmallows.

It's really up to you, so use your imagination…

MEAT
AND POULTRY

PERFECT PRIME RIB
and baked potatoes with chive cream

In France, I make this with a cut called côte de boeuf, but you'll get the same result with thick-cut, bone-in, prime rib steaks. When I'm having meat, I don't necessarily want it to be only rare or medium, I also want some that is well-browned on the outside. With a côte de boeuf or prime rib steak, you can get all that.

FOR 2 BIG EATERS

8 tablespoons thick fresh cream

fresh chives, finely chopped

2–4 large potatoes, washed but not peeled

2 prime rib steaks or 1 côte de boeuf

fine salt

fine white pepper

freshly ground black pepper, to serve

salt flakes or ground sea salt, to serve

- Place the cream in a small bowl. Stir in the chives and set aside in the fridge.
- Tuck the potatoes around the coals when you light the fire (they will take about 40 minutes). Turn them every 10 minutes. Even if the skin turns a little black, the insides will be nicely cooked. When the potatoes are almost done, start cooking the meat.
- Put each steak on a chopping board and hit it with your fist to flatten it slightly and make it easier to cook. (It will regain its shape later on.) Season well with fine salt and fine white pepper, including the fat.
- Place the steaks on the hot grid, above hot coals. After 5 minutes, check the meat. When it no longer sticks to the grid and has a lovely brown crust, turn it over and cook for 4–5 minutes on the other side. When you have a nice crust on both sides, pick up each steak with tongs and roll the fat side against the grid, until all the fat is cooked and crispy.
- Spread the coals to lower the temperature a little. Put the steaks back on the grid. Press the centre of the meat with your finger; if it feels very soft, it isn't cooked enough. Leave for a further 3–4 minutes per side, until done to your liking.
- Remove the steaks from the heat, place on a chopping board, cover with a clean cloth and leave to rest for 10 minutes before slicing. Garnish with pepper and salt flakes. Serve with the potatoes, split in half and filled with the chive cream.

ENTRECÔTE STEAKS
with a green salad and braaied potatoes

If you don't have the time, or don't want to braai a prime rib (côte de boeuf), then an entrecôte or deboned rib-eye steak is the 'fast food' version (but no-one will complain!). The thinner the steak, the faster it will cook.

SERVES 4

8–12 medium potatoes, unpeeled

olive oil, for brushing

sea salt and ground black pepper

1 small red onion, peeled and finely chopped

5 tablespoons balsamic vinegar

fine salt

8 tablespoons olive oil

4 drops toasted sesame oil (optional)

4 baby gem lettuces

4 entrecôtes or rib-eye steaks

fine salt and fine white pepper

salt flakes

freshly ground black pepper

🔥 Boil the potatoes until just tender when pierced with a skewer (do this ahead of time). Cut them into thick slices. Brush with olive oil and season with salt and ground black pepper to taste. Set aside until ready to cook.

🔥 To make the salad, place the red onion in a serving bowl with the balsamic vinegar and a pinch of salt. Stir until the salt dissolves (it may not dissolve completely). After 10 minutes, add the olive oil and a few drops of sesame oil, if using. Stir to combine. Separate the baby gem lettuces into individual leaves and add them to the bowl, but don't toss with the dressing until you are ready to serve.

🔥 Set the grid over very hot coals. Season the steaks with fine salt and fine white pepper and place them on the grid, surrounded by slices of potato. (Turn the potatoes from time to time, until they are golden and crisp around the edges).

🔥 Cook the steaks for 4–6 minutes on one side. When they are golden-brown and don't stick to the grid, turn them and cook for a further 3 minutes on the other side (they should be pink in the centre).

🔥 Serve the steaks with the 'more grilled' side on top, with the tossed salad and grilled potatoes. Garnish with salt flakes and freshly ground black pepper to taste.

VEAL CHOPS
with creamed shallots

What I love about this recipe is that one doesn't expect a dish with a cream sauce at a braai. This dish is very easy to prepare and you can't really go wrong. Just be careful not to cook the meat for too long. You can cook any thin piece of meat this way.

SERVES 2

2 shallots
or small onions, peeled
4 tablespoons thick fresh cream
fine salt and fine white pepper
2 veal chops
sea salt or salt flakes
freshly ground black pepper

- For the shallots, cut four large pieces of heavyweight foil, to make two double-layered parcels. Slice the shallots thinly lengthways. Put each sliced shallot in the centre of one foil square with half the cream. Season to taste. Close the foil parcels very tightly, folding over the edges several times. Place the parcels on the grid, above the coals, and cook for 20 minutes, then place them on the side of the grid to keep warm while you cook the chops.

- Season the veal chops with salt and pepper and place them in the centre of the grid, over the coals. Cook for 4–6 minutes, until they are nicely browned and don't stick to the grid. Turn the chops over and cook for a further 3 minutes on the other side (the meat should be pink in the centre).

- Present the chops with the 'more grilled' side on top. Spoon over the creamed shallots and finish with salt flakes and ground black pepper to taste.

VEAL BREAST
with flat beans

When I'm making giant barbecues, I often prepare pork belly. When I was searching for an alternative to that cut of meat, I discovered veal breast. Ever since, I've been cooking it in large quantities and everyone loves it. It's not quite as tender as a veal chop, but it's more flavourful.

SERVES 4

VINAIGRETTE

2 tablespoons walnut oil or hazelnut oil

4 tablespoons olive oil

2 teaspoons red wine vinegar

zest of 1 lemon

fine salt and fine white pepper

VEAL BREAST

a few walnuts, for serving

2 handfuls flat (runner) beans

1 kg veal breast, sliced ±2 cm thick

fine salt and fine white pepper

pink peppercorns (optional)

- Prepare the vinaigrette by combining the oils with the vinegar, lemon zest, fine salt and white pepper to taste. Set aside.
- Roughly crush the walnuts and toast them lightly in a dry frying pan. Set aside.
- Place the beans directly on the grid, over the coals, and cook for 10–15 minutes, turning frequently until they are just tender and have nice char marks. Move them to the side of the grid to continue cooking slowly while you cook the meat.
- Pat the meat dry with paper towels and season with fine salt and white pepper. Place the meat on the grid over very hot coals. When the slices stop sticking to the grid, turn them over. Do this several times, until the meat is nicely browned on both sides, but still juicy. It should take 10–15 minutes.
- To serve, drizzle the beans with the vinaigrette and sprinkle over the toasted walnuts. Top with the meat and grind over some pink peppercorns.

100% braai BURGERS

Once you've tasted these burgers, you'll always be disappointed with other versions. I think these are the best burgers I've ever had!

SERVES 4

BURGER PATTIES

600 g beef mince

1 onion, finely chopped

½ red pepper, finely chopped

1 pinch chilli powder

Tabasco to taste

sea salt and ground black pepper

TO SERVE

2 tomatoes

1 red onion, peeled and thickly sliced into rings

whole fresh red or green chillies (optional)

4 slices white Cheddar cheese

1–2 sweet pickles, thickly sliced

1 tablespoon Dijon mustard

1 tablespoon tomato sauce

4 burger buns (for homemade braai rolls, see page 118)

🔥 To make the patties, put the meat in the freezer for 30 minutes. Place the chilled mince in a bowl with the onion, red pepper, chilli powder, a few drops of Tabasco and salt and pepper to taste. Combine everything with your hands until well mixed (work quickly, so the meat doesn't heat up). Taste and adjust the seasoning, if necessary. Make four thick burger patties (squeeze them firmly so they hold together). Set aside until ready to cook.

🔥 Place the whole tomatoes directly on the grid along with the onion rings and chillies, if using. When the vegetables are almost cooked, move them to one side of the grid. (Brush or scrape any food residue off the grid so that it is clean before you cook the meat, otherwise the patties will stick.)

🔥 Cook the burgers over hot coals for 5–6 minutes per side, turning regularly. (They need to cook for long enough to cook the onion and pepper in the patties, but don't let the meat dry out.)

🔥 When the patties are almost cooked, place a slice of Cheddar on top of each one. If you want the cheese to melt into the burgers, cover the patties with a large metal bowl.

🔥 Place the buns on the grid for a few minutes, to warm them.

🔥 Put all the ingredients on the table and let everyone build their own burger.

SPATCHCOCKED CHICKEN
with grilled sweetcorn

French people are sometimes scornful about chicken. I find that really surprising, because the chickens you find in France are among the best in the world, with a great choice of breeds and breeding methods. When I first arrived in France, one of the things that surprised me was that chicken tasted of… chicken! However, I find it strange to tie it up to cook it. I suppose it's to make it look pretty. Depending on the quality of the chicken you pick, this dish can be 'gourmet' and sophisticated, or just tasty and delicious.

SERVES 4

1 free-range chicken, spatchcocked

sea salt and ground black pepper

4 sweetcorn cobs, without leaves

1 lime, cut into 4 wedges

- Lightly score the thighs, so they'll cook faster. Season the chicken all over with salt and ground black pepper.

- Place the chicken on a grid above hot coals, with the sweetcorn cobs around it. Cook for about 30 minutes, turning the chicken and the corn from time to time. (Allow the corn to take on some colour, even get a bit burnt. It's delicious this way – you don't even need to add salt or butter to enjoy it.)

- To test whether the chicken is done, lift up a thigh and check if the meat between the thigh and the body is cooked. Prick the breast with the tip of a knife to see if the juices are clear. Place the chicken on a board and cut it into portions. Serve with wedges of lime, for drizzling over the chicken.

To spatchcock a whole chicken, use kitchen scissors to cut along both sides of the backbone and through the skin at the thigh and wing joints. Place your hands on the backbone and press down firmly to flatten it (you'll hear a few small bones breaking).

Spicy CHICKEN WINGS

These crisp, tasty pieces of chicken make a great appetizer. They're the perfect finger food for when you're watching rugby, ideally with a cold beer. To serve chicken wings as an inexpensive main course, allow 5–6 wings per person, with grilled potato wedges and a green salad.

SERVES 4 (AS AN APPETIZER)

8 chicken wings
chilli powder or peri peri powder
sea salt

- Dry the chicken wings with paper towels. Cut the skin at the joints and score the meat at the fleshy end of the wings.
- Season with chilli powder and salt to taste.
- Grill the wings over hot coals, turning them often, as the skin burns quickly. (Use a spatula to flatten the wings so they cook more evenly.)
- When they are cooked through and the skin is crisp, take them off the braai. Separate the wings at the joint and enjoy!

Prepare chicken drumsticks by scoring the meat so you can flatten them, and cook them in the same way.

QUAILS
stuffed with grapes

Surprisingly, this 'gastronomic' dish can be easily prepared on a braai, and it makes a nice surprise. When I arrived in France, I made it to impress my girlfriend, who became my wife.

SERVES 4

1 bunch small white grapes

4 quails, gutted, with the neck on but the head removed

sea salt and ground black pepper

sprigs of fresh thyme

- Place the bunch of grapes on the braai grid and grill for about 10 minutes, turning regularly, until the grapes are golden brown, soft and sweet.
- Dry the insides of the quails with paper towels. Season with salt and pepper, inside and out.
- Stuff each quail with as many cooked grapes as possible (it doesn't matter if some of the grapes burst). Set the leftover grapes aside.
- Make sure the coals are not too hot. Place the sprigs of thyme on the grid and put the quails on top of the thyme. Braai the quails, turning them so you cook both sides of the back first, then both breasts. It should take about 15 minutes for the meat to be cooked through and the skin crispy.
- To serve, open up the quail breasts and add the remaining grilled grapes.

Boneless marinated LAMB SHOULDER WITH FIGS

I often braai the shoulder rather than a leg of lamb, because I find it tastier. When you're cooking a large piece of meat on the braai, slice it in front of your guests. They'll be impressed and enjoy their meal even more.

SERVES 4–6

MARINADE

4 garlic cloves, peeled
1 bunch fresh coriander
1 bunch chives, chopped
1 bunch mint, chopped
¼ green pepper, chopped
1 litre plain yoghurt
sea salt and ground black pepper
1 deboned lamb shoulder
8–12 fresh figs

One day before

- To prepare the marinade, cut the garlic cloves in four, or crush them for a more intense flavour. Set aside a few sprigs of coriander and chop the rest. In a bowl, combine the garlic, herbs, green pepper, yoghurt and salt and pepper to taste. Set aside some of the marinade to serve with the lamb.

- Put the lamb into a large dish and coat it with the rest of the marinade. Cover with cling wrap and place in the fridge.

On the day

- Prepare a fire with a lot of coals (it needs to last a long time). Make sure you keep extra coals on the side to top up the fire.

- Remove the lamb from the marinade and place it on the grid. Cook the lamb for 5–6 minutes, then turn it and brush with the marinade. Repeat this process for about 30 minutes, adding more coals to the braai in order to maintain the temperature.

- When the lamb is almost cooked, stop brushing it with the marinade and allow the skin to brown. Remove it from the grid and leave to rest for 5–6 minutes.

- To cook the figs (it will make them sweeter), place the whole figs on the grid, turning them once or twice. Do this while the meat is resting. (You can also serve them raw.)

- Slice the meat and garnish with sprigs of coriander. Serve with the reserved marinade and the figs, cut in four.

LAMB SPARE RIBS
with braaied artichokes

Lamb ribs are truly delicious; crispy and flavourful. Few people think of cooking artichokes on the braai, but you should try it, you'll be surprised. They take on a slightly charred, smoky flavour and are delicious served alongside these gently spiced ribs. With this dish, everyone gets their hands dirty and enjoys it.

SERVES 4–6 AS AN APPETIZER

RASPBERRY VINAIGRETTE
2 tablespoons raspberry vinegar
2 teaspoons Dijon mustard
fine salt
6 tablespoons oil

RIBS
2 racks of lamb spare ribs
75 g coriander seeds, finely crushed
1 tablespooon sea salt
¼ teaspoon white pepper
¼ teaspoon mild chilli powder
4–6 fresh artichokes, as big as you can get

- To make the vinaigrette, combine the vinegar, mustard and a little salt in a small bowl or jug. Then slowly pour in the oil while stirring constantly. Set aside.

- To prepare the ribs, cut off the thin layer of meat (if there is one) that extends beyond the bones. On the bone side, remove the thin layer of skin with a very sharp knife. Rub the meat with the crushed coriander seeds, sea salt, white pepper and chilli powder. Set aside.

- Prepare the braai with a lot of coals, so you can cook for a long time. When the coals are hot, put the artichokes on the grid. They'll take about an hour to cook. It doesn't matter if the outside gets a little charred.

- After 30–40 minutes, spread out the coals to lower the heat. Place the spare ribs on the grid and cook for about 25 minutes, turning regularly. Make sure to cook the fat until it melts and becomes crispy. When the ribs are ready, cut between the bones with kitchen scissors or a strong knife to separate them.

- Nibble the ribs with your fingers and dip the artichoke leaves in the vinaigrette. At the end, remove the artichoke hearts and chop them into small pieces.

Karoo-style LAMB CHOPS

Karoo lamb has an exceptional flavour. My uncle loved to use his pocket-knife to scrape all the meat from the chop bones (so there was nothing left for the dogs to eat!). He taught me that the best-tasting meat is closest to the bone.

SERVES 4

RUB
150 g coriander seeds
2 tablespoons coarse sea salt
½ teaspoon chilli powder
½ teaspoon white pepper

2–3 lamb loin chops per person

◊ Place all the rub ingredients in a food processor and pulse to combine, or pound in a mortar. (The coriander seeds should be well crushed, but not into a powder.)

◊ Flatten the chops with your hand to make them thinner. Coat them with the rub. Place the cooking grid about 10 cm above the coals. Put the lamb chops on it, and cook, turning a few times, until the outsides become crispy and the meat is cooked all the way through (it should be well cooked, not pink).

Serve the chops with a bulgur salad or grilled baby leeks, and bread cooked on the braai.

For thick-cut chops, coat them with the rub, then line them up on a chopping board, fat-side down and thread them onto one or two pre-soaked skewers. Set the grid at least 20 cm above the coals (this will allow the fat to crisp without overcooking the meat). Stand the chops, fat side down, on the grid and move or turn the skewer until all the fat is well cooked. Take the chops off the braai and remove the skewers. Lower the grid to about 10 cm above the coals. Place the chops flat on the grid and cook for 5 minutes per side, turning once. Serve immediately.

DUCK BREAST
Kapana style

When my family or friends visit me in Paris I like to prepare this dish for them. 'Kapana' is a traditional Namibian way of braaiing, where the meat is sliced on the braai after cooking and several people share it with their fingers. The best way to enjoy this is straight off the fire, when the duck breast is crispy outside and pink and warm inside. If you let the meat rest, it starts to dry out. The goal when cooking duck breast is to melt as much of the fat as possible, so that you only have a thin, crispy layer left. That way, people won't throw away the fat after it has been cooked, as it is very tasty. I slice the duck into bite-sized pieces and serve it with small bowls of salt, pepper or chilli powder for dipping. Eaten with your fingers, it is just perfect!

SERVES 3

1–2 duck breasts
salt flakes or sea salt
ground black pepper
chilli flakes or chilli powder
fresh chives or coriander or your choice of herbs

- Place the duck breast, fat side down, to one side of the grid, where the coals aren't too hot. Cook it slowly for 10–15 minutes, to melt the fat. (The layer of fat will protect the meat and prevent it from overcooking.) When the layer of fat is thin and crispy, remove the breast.
- Wipe the grid with a paper towel. Place the breast, meat side down, in the centre of the grid, where the coals are the hottest. Cook until the meat is crispy and nicely browned (use tongs to turn it so the edges cook, too).
- Remove the breast from the braai and cut it into slices less than 1 cm thick. Serve straight away with salt, ground black pepper, chilli flakes or powder and finely chopped herbs.

Don't score the fat of the breast before cooking, because the meat will start to cook too soon. If necessary, you can score it when you're almost done cooking the fat side, so a little more of the fat runs out.

CARAMELIZED PRIME PORK CHOPS *with Brinjals*

I enjoy braaiing prime pork chops, because they're nice and big and meaty.

SERVES 4

2–4 brinjals, depending on size
4 tablespoons freshly squeezed lemon juice
4 tablespoons soy sauce
4 tablespoons balsamic vinegar
4 pork loin chops
sea salt and ground black pepper
olive oil
lemon wedges

- Place the whole brinjals on the braai grid and cook them for about 30 minutes, turning regularly.
- Combine the lemon juice, soy sauce and balsamic vinegar in a small pan. Place over the heat and reduce until the sauce becomes syrupy.
- Rub the pork chops with salt and pepper and brush them with the warm sauce.
- Place the chops on the grid, over medium coals (if the coals are too hot, the sauce may burn).
- Braai the chops for about 10 minutes, turning them regularly. (If the juice runs clear when you pierce them with the tip of a knife, they're perfect. Don't overcook the chops, as the meat could dry out.)
- Drizzle the remaining sauce over the chops. Cut the brinjals in half, drizzle with olive oil and a few drops of lemon juice, and season with salt and black pepper to taste.

MY SPARE RIBS

I'm crazy about ribs, so I taste them any chance I get, especially when I'm travelling. I love slow-cooked American ribs, where the meat falls off the bones, or the way the Chinese prepare them and, of course, braaied South African spare ribs. I've had some rubbed with spices, others with vinegary sauces, but I prefer them with a slightly sweet sauce, like in this recipe. (If you don't have time to prepare the sauce, use a store-bought yakitori sauce.)

SERVES 4

7 tablespoons soy sauce

100 g brown sugar

4 tablespoons sweet white wine

½ teaspoon onion powder or ½ spring onion, very finely chopped

½ tablespoon lemon zest, or to taste

a few drops Tabasco

1 large rack (±1 kg) of spare ribs

sea salt and ground black pepper to taste

- Prepare enough hot coals to last at least 30 minutes.
- Combine the soy sauce, brown sugar, wine, onion powder, lemon zest and Tabasco in a small pan and reduce until the mixture becomes syrupy. Remove from the braai and reserve.
- If necessary, prepare the ribs by removing the fine membrane on the bone side (they're more pleasant to eat this way) and any skin at the end of the rack.
- Rub the rack well with salt and pepper. If necessary, cut it into pieces to fit on the braai. Place the ribs on the grid and cook, turning regularly, until they're nice and brown. Cook the thickest pieces on all sides. (Lean them against another piece of meat if they won't stand up on their own.)
- When the ribs are almost cooked (after about 20 minutes), start brushing them with the sauce. Be careful, as this sugary sauce burns quite quickly. Turn the ribs often, brushing with sauce every time. The sauce will caramelize, becoming brown and sticky (not black and burnt!).
- Prick a large piece of rib with the tip of a knife. If the juice runs clear, the ribs are ready. Cut between the bones and eat the individual ribs with your fingers.

Asian-style PORK BELLY SANDWICH

I love to eat in the 13th arrondissement in Paris, the Asian neighbourhood. This is where I discovered these sandwiches, in a small shop, with a long queue outside. I loved them and thought they'd be even better when prepared with pork cooked on the braai. This is my recipe.

SERVES 4

2 tablespoons fish sauce (nuoc-nam)

2 tablespoons white vinegar

1 tablespoon lime juice

1 tablespoon castor sugar

4 slices pork belly, cut about 2 cm thick

sea salt and ground black pepper

FOR THE SANDWICHES

2 small baguettes or ciabatta rolls

4 carrots, peeled and coarsely grated

fresh coriander leaves

fresh chilli, deseeded and finely chopped

- In a small bowl, combine the fish sauce, white vinegar and lime juice with the sugar until it is well dissolved. Set aside.
- Dry the slices of pork with paper towels and season them with salt and pepper. Braai for 6–7 minutes over very hot coals, turning often, so they don't burn. The pork should be well cooked and the fat should be crispy, to bring out the flavour. (It doesn't matter if the meat is a little dry because it will be drizzled with sauce.) Cut the meat into bite-sized pieces.
- Cut the baguettes in half lengthways and open them up. Layer the sandwiches with grated carrots, pieces of braaied pork belly, more grated carrots and coriander leaves. Drizzle with sauce, sprinkle with chopped chilli to taste, and close the sandwiches.

Home-made SAUSAGES

Preparing sausages from scratch will earn you the respect of your guests and greatly improve your rating as a braai chef. The goal when cooking these sausages is for the outside to be crispy and the inside still juicy. So don't cook them too fast or too slowly; it's a real balancing act!

MAKES ± 2 KG SAUSAGES

- 2 tablespoons whole coriander seeds
- 650 g beef (not too fatty or dry, chuck steak for example)
- 650 g pork belly
- 650 g breast of lamb
- 2 tablespoons salt
- 2 teaspoons ground white pepper
- 1 teaspoon ground cloves
- ½ teaspoon ground nutmeg
- ½ teaspoon ground mace
- ¼ cup red wine
- 2 m sausage casing (for thick sausages)

- Crush the coriander seeds in a food processor or with a mortar and pestle. Heat them in a dry pan, without oil, to bring out their flavour.
- Cut the meats into large pieces. Grind (mince) them, but not too finely, alternating pieces of beef, pork and lamb.
- Put the ground meat into a bowl with the rest of the ingredients (except the sausage casing) and mix everything rapidly, using your hands. Fry a little of the mixture in a pan and taste it. Adjust the seasoning if necessary.
- Rinse the sausage casing. Fill it up to make one long sausage, then cut it into pieces about 15 cm long (or to your preference). The ends can stay open; they'll turn crispy when you cook them. Don't prick the sausages before cooking. Place them on the grid over coals that are not too hot and cook until done.

CRISPY BEEF RIBS
with grilled baby potatoes

Get your butcher to cut the beef ribs horizontally across four or five bones and about 1 cm thick (depending on the size). Beware of too much fat. I eat two portions; most people eat one.

SERVES 4

baby potatoes, unpeeled

Olive oil

1 bunch fresh parsley, chopped

1–2 portions of ribs per person

fresh garlic cloves, peeled

sea salt and ground black pepper

heavy weights (such as foil-covered bricks)

- Boil the potatoes until just tender. Drain, place in a bowl and toss gently with the olive oil and some of the parsley.
- Rub the meat with garlic cloves and season with sea salt and ground black pepper to taste.
- Position the grid about 10 cm above very hot coals. When the grid is hot, place the ribs on it. They should make a deeply satisfying sizzling sound. Place heavy weights on the ribs.
- Cook the ribs for about 4 minutes, then turn and cook for another 4 minutes on the other side, until cooked and crispy. (The point is to cook the meat fast, so it gets crispy. This is a tasty-but-tough cut of meat that one would normally slow-cook for hours. That's why we slice it thin and cook it fast and well; we get the taste without the tough.) Serve immediately.
- While the ribs are cooking, place the potatoes on the grid alongside them and turn frequently, until they are golden brown. Sprinkle with some more salt and parsley before serving.

Roadside butterflied CHICKEN THIGHS

When I was small, my mother did this as a fast way to cook chicken when we were travelling and had only a limited supply of wood, which gives you intense heat for a short time. In India, they use the same technique when they barbecue chicken in the immensely hot tandoor ovens, but my mom developed this method independently. The thinner the meat, the faster it cooks. Chicken thighs have oily meat, so they remain crisp yet juicy. Don't try this with chicken breasts. Serve with garlicky mushrooms.

SERVES 4–6

- 1–2 chicken thighs per person
- fine salt
- peri peri powder
- 4–6 tablespoons butter
- 2 garlic cloves, peeled and chopped
- 1–2 tablespoons chopped parsley
- black mushrooms

◉ Slice the thighs on the meaty side to the bone, opening them up until you have equal thickness (you'll find that the meat has natural divides you can follow). Season to taste with salt and peri peri powder. (Don't use any oil or sauce; you want them to be crispy.)

◉ Melt the butter in a saucepan over the coals. Add the chopped garlic and parsley and stir to combine. Move the saucepan to one side to keep the mixture warm, but don't let it boil.

◉ Place the thighs on a hot grid close to very hot coals. Turn regularly until nicely charred, but not burnt (this should take no longer than 10 minutes). Serve immediately.

◉ While the chicken is cooking, place the mushrooms, skin side down, on the grid to warm up and get some nice gridlines. Pour over the hot garlic butter and serve with the chicken.

FISH
AND SEAFOOD

WHOLE MULLET
with flatbread

This dish is a winner on all counts. The fish is flavourful, inexpensive and absolutely delicious when served with hot bread straight off the fire! What more could you want?

SERVES 4–6

2 mullets (± 1.5 kg each), gutted but not scaled

basic bread dough (see page 116)

flour, for dusting

butter

◊ Open the mullets' bellies, clean and rinse them. Place the fish on the grid over hot coals. Grill on both sides, turning from time to time, for 20–25 minutes. Place the fish on a chopping board to rest and cook a little more.

◊ To make the flatbreads, prepare the quantity of dough in the basic recipe. Divide the dough into eight to twelve balls, a little smaller than a tennis ball. (If you have too much dough, wrap the surplus in cling wrap and place it in the fridge.) Using a rolling pin or an empty bottle, roll out each ball to a rough circle, about 2 mm thick (make sure there are no holes in the dough). Dust the flatbreads with flour.

◊ Bring the coals together, if necessary, so they are nice and hot. Put the flatbreads on the grid for 20–30 seconds. When they become stiff and stop sticking to the grid, turn them over. After about 15 seconds, a pocket of air will form and they will puff up; they are ready. (If you want them a little browner, turn them over and let them cook a little longer.)

◊ To serve, butter a piece of hot bread and top it with some fish.

TUNA STEAKS
with rice salad

Tuna steaks are quick and easy to prepare, and more importantly, really delicious. They're perfect for guests who drop in at the last minute. Choose good quality, thick tuna steaks that won't dry out when you cook them.

SERVES 4

2 tuna steaks (± 3 cm thick)
olive oil
sea salt and ground black pepper
lemon wedges

RICE SALAD
1 small red pepper
1 carrot
1 red onion
6 tablespoons olive oil
2 tablespoons balsamic vinegar
600 g cold, cooked rice
fresh mint, basil or herbs of your choice
sea salt and ground black pepper

- Dry the tuna steaks with paper towels. Rub them with olive oil and season to taste with sea salt and black pepper.
- To prepare the salad, deseed the red pepper and chop it finely. Peel the carrot and onion and chop them finely. Combine the olive oil with the balsamic vinegar. Add all the salad ingredients to the rice and stir to combine. Add the herbs and season to taste with sea salt and black pepper.
- Place the tuna steaks on the grid over very hot coals. It is important that they cook fast so they stay moist. As soon as they stop sticking to the grid, give them a quarter-turn, on the same side, to make charred diamond shapes.
- Turn the tuna steaks over and cook them the same way on the other side. It should take about 2 minutes per side (tuna should be well grilled on the outside, but almost raw inside, a bit like a rare steak). Remove them immediately from the braai.
- Serve with the rice salad and lemon wedges. (Use sharp knives when eating to avoid mashing the tuna.)

You can add other ingredients, like pieces of avocado or chopped black olives, to the rice salad.

SALMON
with spinach and butternut

In general, I prefer to cook fish whole, but this recipe is best when you don't have enough people around the table to eat a whole salmon. Just make sure you don't overcook the fillets.

SERVES 4

1 butternut

olive oil

4 salmon portions, skin on

sea salt and ground black pepper

baby spinach leaves

lemon wedges

🔥 Halve the butternut and cut it lengthways into 1-cm-thick slices. Lightly coat with olive oil.

🔥 Dry the salmon portions with paper towels and lightly coat with olive oil. Season the salmon and butternut with salt and pepper.

🔥 Prepare a medium-hot fire. Place the butternut on the grid first. Turn the slices regularly. After 10–15 minutes, when the butternut starts to soften, add the salmon, flesh side down.

🔥 As soon as the flesh releases easily from the grid, give the salmon a quarter turn, on the same side, to create diamond-shaped char marks. Cook all three skinless sides the same way. Cook the skin side last (it will take longer because the skin protects the flesh). The salmon should be cooked through but not dry; it should feel moist to the touch, but firmer than when it's raw. Remove the salmon from the braai and leave to rest for 3–5 minutes (don't cover the fish or it will lose its crispness).

🔥 While the salmon rests, throw the spinach on the grid. As soon as it wilts, remove it.

🔥 Serve the salmon, butternut and spinach with a squeeze of lemon juice and a drizzle of olive oil.

GRILLED OCTOPUS
with origanum

I learned to cook octopus as a young boy, when I went fishing. Many fish eat small crabs; so do octopus. To catch the crabs we used as bait, we'd first catch an octopus by hand and tie a noose around its 'neck' before plunging it into a rock pool. The scared crabs would get out as fast as possible, making it super-easy to catch them! When we'd gathered enough crabs, we'd string up the octopus so we could grill it in the evening, after we'd finished fishing.

SERVES 4

1 octopus (with tentacles no thicker than 3–4 cm)
olive oil
dried origanum
salt flakes or sea salt
lime wedges

Two days before

🔥 Turn the 'head' of the octopus inside out and remove its intestines and slide your fingers inside to remove the beak. (You can ask your fishmonger to do this.) Wash the octopus well and dry with paper towels. Hang it upside down to dry for 24 hours. When the octopus is dry, it is ready for the braai.

On the day

🔥 Cut off the tentacles and place them on a grid quite high above the coals (about 15 cm). Braai gently for about 30 minutes.

🔥 Cut the pouch ('head') so you can flatten it by hand. Place it on the grid; it will cook faster than the tentacles because it is thinner. When the tip of a knife penetrates the flesh easily, brush the pieces of octopus with olive oil and sprinkle with origanum. Continue cooking, turning the pieces over once or twice, until they are done.

🔥 Use a sharp knife to cut the octopus into pieces. Garnish to taste with salt, origanum, lime juice and a drizzle of olive oil.

Serve with wedges of fresh tomato and braaied baby potatoes.

SEA BASS
with garlic butter

Sea bass is the French fish most like the South African yellowtail that I used to catch while freediving at Agulhas. If you have any leftovers, it's delicious cold, reheated, or in fishcakes.

SERVES 4–6

1 whole head of garlic

1 lemon

6 tablespoons butter

sea salt and ground black pepper

1 whole sea bass or yellowtail or Cape salmon (± 2 kg), neither gutted nor scaled

◊ Cut the head of garlic in half through the centre and cut the lemon into thick slices. Braai the garlic and lemon briefly, to bring out the flavours. Put them into a flameproof pan with the butter, salt and black pepper, and melt the butter slowly.

◊ To butterfly the fish, use a sharp knife to cut along the backbone, from head to tail, then open it out, keeping both sides attached. Gut the fish and remove the gills. Then rinse it and dry with paper towels. Lie the fish flat in a hinged grid and place it, flesh-side down, over very hot coals. Cook for about 5 minutes, until the flesh is nicely browned.

◊ Spread the coals to reduce the heat. Turn the grid and cook the fish on the skin side for 10–15 minutes, brushing the flesh a few times with the flavoured butter.

Serve with a tomato salad and the extra garlic butter on the side.

BLACK MUSSELS
au naturel

When we went fishing, we always had a braai grid and some wood in the car. If we came back empty handed, we'd simply pick some mussels off the rocks at low tide. Don't pick mussels that grow along the bottom of the rocks because they'll be sandy. I love black mussels cooked on an open fire and served with a squeeze of citrus, and a glass of cold Chardonnay. The good life!

**SERVES 4
(AS A MAIN COURSE)**

4 litres whole black mussels

**4 clementines or oranges
(optional)**

- Choose a braai grid that the mussels can't fall through; you don't want them ending up in the fire. Prepare a thick layer of very hot coals. Black mussels need to cook quickly, otherwise they could put out the fire because they lose water when they open.
- Spread the mussels on the grid. Cover them with a large metal bowl, or close the lid of a kettle braai.
- Cut the clementines or oranges in half and braai them, cut side down, alongside the mussels. They'll refresh your palate when you're eating the mussels.
- As soon as the mussels open up they're ready to eat. Try them 'au naturel'; they really taste of the sea. (Discard any mussels that don't open.) Use an empty shell as a pincer to pick out the mussel flesh. Enjoy!

GRILLED CRAYFISH
with sumac butter

This is a dish that you can prepare on the braai for a truly special occasion.

SERVES 2

6 tablespoons butter

2 pinches ground sumac or a little lemon juice

2 whole crayfish (± 300 g each), split and with the entrails removed

- Prepare a very hot fire.
- Melt the butter and sumac together in a small flameproof pan.
- Place the crayfish in a hinged grid to make it easier to turn them, or place them directly on the grid. Cook, flesh-side down, for about 4 minutes, until nicely browned.
- Spread the coals to reduce the heat. Turn the crayfish and baste the flesh with the sumac butter.
- Cook the crayfish over a low heat for about 10 minutes, basting from time to time (reserve some melted butter for serving). When the tip of a knife pierces the flesh easily, they are ready. Serve with the remaining sumac butter on the side.

Sumac is a lemony-flavoured spice that is used in Middle Eastern and Southeast Asian cooking.

SIDE DISHES,
VEGETABLES, FRUITS AND BREADS

Garlic BRINJALS

For me there are two kinds of people: those who love brinjals and those who don't. I have to confess that I'm part of the second group. It has to be said, though, that it is the vegetable that contains the most histamine, and I think I'm a little allergic. However, my friends who like brinjals think this is the best way to eat them. The smoky flavour of the brinjal and the sweetness of the cooked garlic make a perfect combination! Your vegetarian and vegan friends will enjoy this recipe.

SERVES 4

2 large brinjals
2 heads of garlic
olive oil
sea salt and ground black pepper
lemon wedges

- As soon as the fire is lit, place the whole brinjals and the unpeeled heads of garlic on the grid and let them cook for about 45 minutes, turning from time to time (their skin will stop them from burning). The garlic will be ready first. As soon as the flesh feels soft, remove the heads, separate the cloves and squeeze the cooked pulp into a bowl, mashing it with a fork.

- The brinjals are cooked when they are soft and collapsing. Cut them in half and, without damaging the skins, scoop out the flesh with a spoon, placing it in the bowl with the garlic.

- Using a fork, lightly mash the brinjal and garlic with a little olive oil. Season to taste with sea salt and black pepper.

- Pile the mixture into the brinjal skins. Serve with wedges of lemon on the side.

BRUSSELS SPROUTS, *cauliflower and Swiss chard*

This isn't really a recipe. I just want to show that you can cook these vegetables on the braai, which will make a change from your usual side dishes. When I was young, we braaied meat or fish several times a week, but vegetables were always cooked in the kitchen. When I started barbecuing professionally, I experimented with grilling vegetables and now I've become a fan. Try it with all the vegetables you like; just make sure they don't fall through the grid!

Brussels sprouts
cauliflower, cut into wedges
olive oil or melted butter
Swiss chard, washed
sea salt and ground black pepper
soy sauce

- Place the whole Brussels sprouts and the cauliflower wedges directly on the grid.
- Cook for about 30 minutes in total, turning and basting frequently with olive oil or melted butter until they are tender and nicely browned.
- After about 10 minutes, add the Swiss chard. (I tie the leaves into a bundle so they stay together). Cook for about 20 minutes, turning frequently.
- To serve, season the Brussels sprouts and cauliflower with sea salt and black pepper and serve with extra olive oil or melted butter on the side. Add a dash of soy sauce to the Swiss chard, to bring out the flavour.

Potato and CARROT PAPILLOTES

Papillotes (pronounced papi-jots) is the French word for food folded and baked in a parcel. It sounds a lot better than parcel, so use it! Instead of individual parcels, you can prepare one large papillote; just add 15 minutes to the cooking time.

FOR 4 PARCELS

4 large potatoes
4 carrots
2 onions
4 tablespoons butter
sea salt and fine white pepper

- Peel the potatoes, carrots and onions.
- Cut the potatoes and carrots into 2-cm cubes and roughly chop the onions.
- Cut 4 large sheets of parchment or greaseproof paper. Place a quarter of the vegetables on each sheet, dot with butter and season to taste. Fold the paper to enclose the *papillotes*, then wrap each one in heavyweight foil, sealing them well.
- Place the *papillotes* on the grid and cook for 30–45 minutes, turning frequently. The vegetables will be slightly caramelized and their flavours will come together.

SWEET POTATO PAPILLOTES
with ginger and orange

The flavours of orange and ginger give sweet potato some zing. These slightly sweet vegetables are delicious with lamb or fish.

SERVES 4

2 large sweet potatoes
1 orange
2 thumb-sized pieces of fresh ginger
2 tablespoons brown sugar
4 tablespoons butter
salt and fine white pepper

- Peel the sweet potatoes and cut them lengthways into thick slices (at most 1 cm thick).
- Wash and dry the orange, but don't peel it. Cut it into slices about 0.5 cm-thick.
- Peel and grate the fresh ginger.
- Cut 4 large sheets of parchment or greaseproof paper. Place a quarter of the ingredients on each sheet, dot with butter and season to taste. Fold the paper to enclose the *papillotes*, then wrap each one in heavyweight foil, sealing them well.
- Place the *papillotes* on the grid and cook for about 30 minutes, turning from time to time.

Braaied whole BUTTERNUT

Butternut is ideal for the braai. I cook it often and you'll find it in several of my recipes. To me, it has a truly delicious flavour and is the best variety of squash. Even if you don't like pumpkin, you'll love butternut. On top of that, it's beautiful and easy to prepare. You can cook it many ways: in slices, in a papillote… My favourite is keeping it whole, like in this recipe.

SERVES 2–4

1 butternut squash
4 tablespoons butter
salt and fine white pepper
fresh thyme

- Put the whole, unpeeled butternut on the grid as soon as you start the fire. (If you need to make space for other ingredients later on, you can place the butternut directly on the coals, but remember to wipe the skin clean before serving it.)
- Cook for 30–45 minutes, turning from time to time, until the flesh is soft when pressed, or pierced with the tip of a knife.
- When the butternut is cooked, cut it in half lengthways and scoop out the seeds, if desired. Add 1–2 tablespoons of butter to each half. Season with salt and pepper and sprinkle with thyme.

Butternut skin is edible, so you don't have to remove the flesh to eat it. You can simply slice the butternut and enjoy it!

BANANAS
with chocolate and cream

This is the easiest dessert to prepare. On top of that, everyone loves it. It doesn't matter whether it is under- or overcooked, you can't go wrong!

SERVES 4

4 large, ripe bananas

50 g dark chocolate, broken into pieces

4 tablespoons thick fresh cream

- As soon as you have finished cooking your main course on the braai, place the whole, unpeeled bananas over a low heat. As the skin is very thick, it doesn't matter if you forget about them while you are eating. But if you do think about them, turn them over once or twice. Leave the bananas to cook until they are soft and the skin is completely black. (They are not burnt, it's just that the skin changes colour when they cook.)
- When the bananas are almost ready, melt the chocolate in a small saucepan on the braai. Keep an eye on it.
- Cut the cooked bananas in two, or split the skin and leave them whole. Pour the cream and the melted chocolate over the bananas and eat them with a spoon.

You can also serve the bananas with cinnamon-sugar or ice cream or drizzle them with a little brandy or rum blended with some fresh cream to mellow the taste.

Spicy PINEAPPLE

I got the idea for this when I was making a film in Mauritius. There were people on the beach selling raw pineapple sprinkled with chilli. I found the combination of flavours really interesting, so I created a hot version, because I love pineapple when it gets a smoky, grilled taste from the braai. The wedges don't need much attention while they are cooking, so you can cook them at the end of the meal, but prepare the rum-flavoured cream ahead of time.

SERVES 4

WHIPPED CREAM WITH RUM

¾ cup very cold whipping cream

1 teaspoon white rum

1 drop vanilla extract

2 teaspoons icing sugar

1 pineapple

2 tablespoons brown sugar

1 teaspoon chilli powder (or to taste)

1 teaspoon salt

- Whisk the cream until firm. Add the rum and vanilla extract, then gently fold in the icing sugar. Place in the fridge until ready to serve.
- Quarter the pineapple (or cut it into wedges if it is very big).
- Combine the sugar, chilli powder and salt and sprinkle the mixture over the wedges.
- Place the pineapple, flesh side down, on the grid, about 10 cm above the coals. Cook for 5–10 minutes, turning several times, until the flesh starts to caramelize. Serve the warm pineapple with the chilled rum-flavoured cream.

GRILLED GRAPES
with vanilla and nuts

This original recipe will surprise your guests. This rich and sweet dessert is a true delight.

SERVES 4

1–2 bunches large, thick-skinned, white grapes

2 vanilla pods

1 cup thick fresh cream

4 tablespoons runny honey

walnuts (whole or roughly crushed)

◊ Place the bunches of grapes on the braai grid over a low heat. Turn regularly (holding them by the stem), until the grapes are golden brown.

◊ While the grapes are cooking, split the vanilla pods down the centre and scrape out the seeds. Stir them into the fresh cream.

◊ When the grapes are ready, put them on a platter and serve with the vanilla cream, honey and the crushed walnuts.

Basic BREAD DOUGH

I use this dough for several recipes in this book. It's easier to knead the dough in a food processor, but this is the method for making it by hand.

MAKES 1 LOAF OR 10 ROLLS

1 kg white bread flour, plus a little extra for your hands

20 g salt

2–2½ cups lukewarm water

5 g baker's yeast

1 teaspoon castor sugar

- Combine the flour and salt in a large bowl.
- Pour 1½ cups of lukewarm water into a smaller bowl and add the yeast and sugar. Stir until everything is dissolved. Wait for the mixture to start foaming a little. Stir in another ¾ cup of lukewarm water. Add the yeast mixture to the flour, stirring with a large spoon.
- Knead the dough with your hands until it becomes smooth and elastic. It takes quite a while. If you stretch the dough, you should be able to see through it without tearing it.
- Place the dough back in the bowl, cover with a clean cloth and leave to rest for 20–30 minutes in a warm place until it has doubled in size.
- Flour your hands and press down on the dough to get rid of any air bubbles. Shape the dough into one round ball or 10 round or oval rolls. Cover with a clean cloth and leave to rise for a further 20–30 minutes before cooking. (The dough will keep for a few days in the fridge, covered in cling wrap.)

Bake braai rolls (see page 118) in the oven at 180 °C for 20 minutes, or over the coals for about 20 minutes, turning them regularly until they sound hollow when you tap them. If you cook them ahead of time, you can reheat them in the oven when you're ready to eat.

BRAAI ROLLS

No braai is complete without these bread rolls. You can use them for making burgers, for dipping in the meat juices or just to go with dishes you've cooked on the braai. You can also serve them with butter and jam as a dessert. But don't wait to eat them; they're best when they are hot.

FOR 10 ROLLS

bread dough (see page 116)
flour, for dusting

- Prepare the quantity of bread dough in the basic recipe. (If you have too much dough, keep the surplus in the fridge, covered in cling wrap.)
- Make balls the size of a large fist. Flour them well and flatten each ball by hand to a thickness of 4 cm (or 1 cm, if you're making burger buns).
- Place the disks of dough on a clean, dry grid over not-too-hot coals and braai until the bottom starts to brown and harden. Turn them and continue cooking until the other side is also nice and brown. (If the rolls stick to the grid, wait a little before turning them.)
- At this point, the bread isn't ready yet. Turn it over again. You can even cook the edges. You'll know that it is cooked if it rings hollow when you knock it.

GARLIC BREAD
with herbs

Just thinking about the irresistible smell of this bread when you open the parcel makes my mouth water.

SERVES 6

50 g softened butter

2 garlic cloves, peeled and crushed

salt and fine white pepper

1 baguette (French loaf)

a few sprigs of thyme, rosemary, or herbs of your choice

- Combine the butter with the crushed garlic and salt and pepper to taste.
- Slice the baguette without detaching the slices, so that it stays whole.
- Spread the garlic butter between the slices. Top with sprigs of fresh herbs.
- Wrap the bread in greaseproof paper or heavyweight foil, making sure the parcel is tightly closed (tie it with kitchen string, if necessary).
- Place the wrapped bread on the grid and cook for about 20 minutes, turning regularly.
- To serve, open the parcel and remove the herbs. Cut through the slices of bread to separate them.

CORN BREAD

This isn't a braai recipe, but I love this moist, golden bread so much, and I think it goes so well with braaied dishes, that I wanted to share the recipe with you.

FOR 1 LOAF

- 400 g can whole kernel corn (not creamed sweetcorn)
- 2 eggs
- 125 g flour
- 125 g cornflour (Maizena)
- 50 g castor sugar
- 1 teaspoon baking powder
- 1 teaspoon salt
- 2 tablespoons water
- butter or oil, for greasing

- In a blender or food processor, process half the canned corn with its liquid until smooth.
- Add the remaining corn and process briefly (you want to retain some texture).
- Combine the dry ingredients in a mixing bowl.
- Add the corn, plus 2 tablespoons of water, and mix well.
- Pour the dough into a well-greased loaf tin or round cake tin.
- Bake in a preheated oven at 180°C for about 1½ hours, until the bread is golden brown and the tip of a knife comes out clean.
- Leave the bread to cool in the tin before turning out and serving.

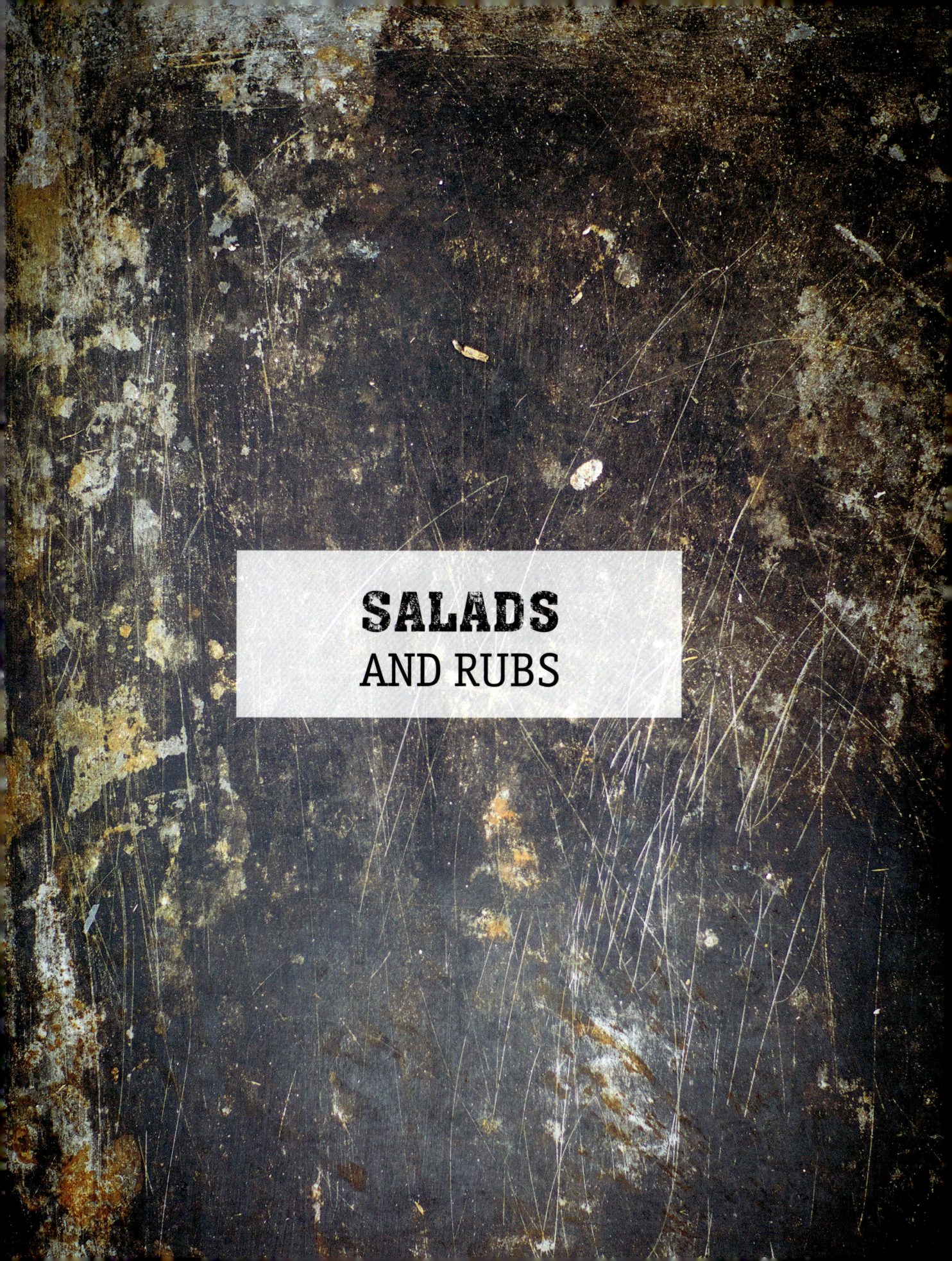
SALADS
AND RUBS

BRAAIED VEGETABLES
with garlic vinaigrette

This isn't really a recipe. It's more of a way to prepare a tasty salad with the vegetables you like to braai. You can serve it as a starter or as a side dish.

SERVES 4

GARLIC VINAIGRETTE
2 tablespoons balsamic vinegar
1 teaspoon Dijon mustard
sea salt and ground black pepper
6 tablespoons olive oil

VEGETABLES
1 head garlic, unpeeled
green, red or yellow peppers
baby marrows
brinjals, halved
butternut, cut into wedges
red onions, peeled
tomatoes (halved, if big)
finely chopped chives or other herbs

- To make the vinaigrette, combine the vinegar and mustard in a jug or small bowl. Season with salt and pepper to taste, then slowly add the oil, stirring constantly, until the vinaigrette is smooth. Set aside.
- Place a grid over the hot coals. Place the whole, unpeeled head of garlic on the grid.
- Braai the peppers, turning them frequently until the skin blackens and blisters. Set aside to cool, until you can use your fingers to peel away the skin.
- Meanwhile, place all the other vegetables on the grid and cook, turning as necessary, until they are soft but not mushy. Remove each one when it is ready.
- Slice the vegetables or cut them into bite-sized chunks and place them in a serving dish.
- Squeeze the warm pulp from the garlic cloves and add it to the vinaigrette. Pour the garlic vinaigrette over the warm vegetables and stir gently to combine. Sprinkle with chopped chives.

POTATO *salad*

As there is more vinegar than oil in the dressing, it will sink to the bottom of the salad bowl rather than coating the ingredients, so turn the salad well before serving.

SERVES 4

VINAIGRETTE

¾ cup of vinegar from the pickles (see below)

1 tablespoon Dijon mustard

sea salt and ground black pepper

6 tablespoons canola oil or sunflower oil

12 medium-sized potatoes

4 sweet pickles or gherkins

1 red onion

fresh flat-leaf parsley or coriander leaves

- To make the vinaigrette, combine the vinegar and mustard in a jug or small bowl. Season with salt and pepper to taste, then slowly add the oil, stirring constantly, until the vinaigrette is smooth. Set aside.
- Wash the potatoes and boil them until they are just soft when pierced with the tip of a knife. Run them under cold water to cool them. You can leave the skin on or remove it, as you like. Cut the potatoes into halves or quarters.
- Chop the pickles into small dice.
- Peel the onion and slice it finely.
- Place the potatoes, onion and pickles in a salad bowl. When ready to serve, pour over the vinaigrette. Mix gently and garnish with fresh herbs.

BULGUR SALAD
with apricots and peaches

Before I arrived in France, I'd never cooked bulgur, although I'd tasted it during my travels. For a more local flavour, you can make this with pearled wheat ('stampkoring') instead of bulgur.

SERVES 4

100 g uncooked bulgur

6 canned apricot halves

2 canned peach halves

2–4 soft-dried apricots (optional)

1 shallot or spring onion, peeled and thinly sliced

chopped chives or fresh mint

DRESSING

8 tablespoons canola or sunflower oil

4 tablespoons syrup from the apricots

4 tablespoons syrup from the peaches

juice of 1 lemon

sea salt and ground black pepper

- Cook the bulgur or pearled wheat according to the instructions on the packet. Drain and leave to cool. (Pearled wheat needs to be cooked for longer; bulgur is pre-cooked.)
- Cut the fruit into small pieces, reserving a few larger pieces for garnish.
- To make the dressing, combine all the ingredients in a jug or small bowl, adjusting the combination of ingredients to taste.
- Place the cooled bulgur in a serving dish. Add the chopped fruit, sliced shallot and chopped herbs. Pour over the dressing and stir to combine.
- Top with the reserved fruit garnish and place in the fridge for a few hours.
- Scatter over some extra herbs before serving.

TOMATO *salad*

This is one of my favourite salads. Don't add any vinegar. Prepare it the way they do in Greece, with only olive oil. It is very important that your tomatoes are ripe and tasty and that you use a good quality extra-virgin olive oil. An easy way to find out if your tomatoes are flavourful is to smell them. If they smell good, they are good. Serve this salad with good bread to dip into the delicious juices from the tomatoes.

SERVES 4

- an assortment of different fresh tomatoes
- 1 white onion
- fresh chives or basil leaves
- 2 tablespoons extra-virgin olive oil
- sea salt and ground black pepper

- Slice or quarter the tomatoes, depending on their size.
- Peel the onion and slice it thinly.
- Chop the herbs.
- Spread everything on a serving platter. Drizzle with olive oil and season to taste with salt and pepper.

BEETROOT AND ONION
salad

I enjoy this sweet-and-sour salad with many of the dishes I cook on the braai. I usually serve it in individual small bowls so the beetroot doesn't stain the other food on my plate. It is even better when made a few days ahead, to allow all the flavours to come together. Keep it in the fridge and gently stir from time to time.

SERVES 4

4 medium-sized cooked beetroots
1 small white onion
¾ cup white vinegar
2 tablespoons castor sugar
salt and fine white pepper

- Peel the beetroots and slice them thinly.
- Peel the onion and slice it into thin rings.
- Place the beetroot and onion in a shallow salad bowl.
- Combine the vinegar and sugar in a small bowl. Add salt and pepper to taste and stir until the sugar is dissolved. Drizzle the dressing over the beetroot and onion and toss gently to coat. Leave to rest in the fridge for at least an hour before serving.

To cook raw beetroots, boil or steam them until they are soft. This can take a while, depending on their size.

RUBS

Rubs are dry mixtures of spices, herbs and flavourings. The difference between a rub and a seasoning is that rubs flavour the food rather than just enhance its taste. You can rub food just before cooking, but if you've got time, do it a few hours ahead. Don't be shy, experiment with your own flavour combinations!

BASIC RUB

This goes with almost every kind of food.

150 g coarse sea salt, lightly ground
50 g light brown sugar
30 g ground paprika
3 tablespoons ground black pepper
1 tablespoon garlic flakes
1 tablespoon onion flakes
½ teaspoon cayenne pepper

Combine all the ingredients.

HERB RUB

This goes especially well with fish.

4 tablespoons dried basil
4 tablespoons dried rosemary
2 tablespoons dried origanum
2 tablespoons dried thyme
2 bay leaves, finely crumbled
1 teaspoon fine white pepper
1 teaspoon ground coriander
½ teaspoon ground cloves

Combine all the ingredients.

CORIANDER RUB

Delicious with lamb and beef.

150 g coriander seeds
2 tablespoons coarse sea salt, lightly ground
½ teaspoon chilli flakes
½ teaspoon fine white pepper

Whiz the ingredients in a food processor or crush them in a mortar.

SPICY RUB

Use with poultry and pork.

150 g coarse sea salt, lightly ground
50 g ground paprika
3 tablespoons ground black pepper
1 tablespoon cayenne pepper
1 tablespoon dried thyme
1 tablespoon onion flakes
1 tablespoon garlic flakes
2 teaspoons fine white pepper
1 bay leaf, finely crumbled

Combine all the ingredients.

GINGER-CURRY RUB

This goes with everything.

300 g castor sugar
4 teaspoons coarse sea salt, lightly ground
2 tablespoons ground turmeric
1 teaspoon ground ginger
1 teaspoon mild curry powder
1 teaspoon fine white pepper
1 teaspoon cayenne pepper
1 teaspoon ground mace
1 teaspoon ground allspice
1 teaspoon ground coriander
1 teaspoon dried rosemary, crumbled

Combine all the ingredients.

INDEX

Artichokes, braaied 60
Asian-style pork belly sandwich 70

Bananas with chocolate and cream 110
Basic bread dough 116
Beef 42, 44, 50, 74
Beetroot and onion salad 136
Black mussels au naturel 92
Boneless marinated lamb shoulder with figs 58
Braai burgers 50
Braai rolls 118
Braaied vegetables with garlic vinaigrette 128
Braaied whole butternut 108
Bread 32, 34, 70, 82, 116, 118, 120, 122
Brinjals 66, 100
Brussels sprouts, cauliflower and Swiss chard 102
Bulgur salad with apricots and peaches 132
Burgers 50
Butternut 86, 108

Caramelized prime pork chops with brinjals 66
Chicken 24, 52, 54, 76
    see also Poultry
Chops 46, 62, 66
Corn bread 122
Côte de boeuf 42, 44
Crispy beef ribs with grilled baby potatoes 74
Curried chicken sosaties 24

Desserts 36, 110, 112
Dressings 48, 60, 128, 130, 132
Duck breast Kapana style 64

Entrecote steaks with a green salad and braaied potatoes 44
Flatbread, *see* Bread

Fish 82, 84, 86, 90
    see also Seafood
Fruit 56, 112, 114

Garlic bread with herbs 120
Garlic brinjals 100
Grilled crayfish with sumac butter 94
Grilled grapes with vanilla and nuts 114
Grilled octopus with origanum 88

Home-made sausages 72

Karoo-style lamb chops 62
Kebabs, *see* Skewers
Kidney 26

Lamb 26, 28, 58, 60, 62
Lamb spare ribs with braaied artichokes 60
Liver 26

Marshmallows, braaied 36
Mushroom skewers 32
My spare ribs 68

Papillotes 104, 106
Parcels, *see* Papillotes
Perfect prime rib and baked potatoes with chive cream 42
Peri peri prawns 30
Pork 66, 68, 70
    see also Sausage
Potato and carrot papillotes 104
Potato salad 130
Potatoes 42, 44, 74, 104, 106, 130
Poultry 56, 64
Prawns 30

Quails stuffed with grapes 56

Ribs, beef 74
Rice salad 84

Roadside butterflied chicken thighs 76
Rubs 138

S'mores 36
Salads 84, 128, 130, 132, 134, 136
    see also Vegetables
Salmon with spinach and butternut 86
Sausages 28, 72
Sea bass with garlic butter 90
Seafood 30, 88, 92, 94
    see also Fish
Shallots, creamed 46
Skewers 24, 26, 28, 30, 32, 34, 36
Skinless coriander sausages 28
Sosaties 24
Spare ribs 68
    see also Ribs
Spatchcocked chicken with grilled sweetcorn 52
Spicy chicken wings 54
Spicy pineapple 112
Stampkoring, *see* Bulgur
Steak, *see* Beef
Stick bread 34
Sticks, *see* Skewers
Sweet and sour lamb kidney and liver skewers 26
Sweet and sour mushroom skewers 32
Sweet potato papillotes with ginger and orange 106

Tomato salad 134
Tuna steaks with rice salad 84

Veal breast with flat beans 48
Veal chops with creamed shallots 46
Vegetables 32, 42, 44, 46, 48, 52, 66, 74, 84, 86, 100, 102, 103, 104, 106, 108, 128
Vegetables, *see also* Salads
Vinaigrette, *see* Dressings

Whole mullet with flatbread 82

Dedication

To my ever-forbearing, though much entertained, mother, Neelsie, the one constant in our lives. She has been a rock-solid support throughout all of my most quixotic obsessions, some of which turned into triumphs.
Dankie moederlief.

Aknowledgements

I want to thank my dear friend and fellow intrepid food adventurer, Jan Hendrik van der Westhuizen, who took most of the gorgeous pictures in this book. He is a multi-talented, cross-disciplinary genius – a boerseun who conquered cuisine in France and was the first South African to be honoured with a Michelin star. Watch him go!

Thanks also to the indefatiguable Inemari, who was our right hand during the photo shoot and generously shared her ouma's cornbread recipe.

First published in the English language in 2018 by Struik Lifestyle,
an imprint of Penguin Random House South Africa (Pty) Ltd
Company Reg. No. 1953/000441/07
The Estuaries, 4 Oxbow Crescent, Century Avenue, Century City 7441
PO Box 1144, Cape Town, 8000, South Africa
www.penguinrandomhouse.co.za

Published originally under the title *Champion du barbecue*
© 2016 by Editions Solar, Department of Place des Editeurs, Paris
English translation: Copyright © 2018, Penguin Random House South Africa (Pty) Ltd
Copyright © in photographs: Editions Solar, with the exception of the following:
front cover © Jan Hendrik van der Westhuizen; pages 75 and 77 © Kobus Botha.

All rights reserved. No part of this publication may be reproduced, stored in a retrieval system or transmitted, in any form or by any means, electronic, mechanical, photocopying, recording or otherwise, without the prior written permission of the publishers and the copyright holders.

English language edition
Publisher: Linda de Villiers
Managing editor: Cecilia Barfield
Design manager: Beverley Dodd
Typesetter: Randall Watson
Translator: Nicole Seeman
Editor: Gill Gordon
Proofreader: Roelien Theron
Photographers: Jan Hendrik van der Westhuizen, Kobus Botha
Food stylist: Inemari Rabie

Reproduction by Hirt & Carter Cape (Pty) Ltd
Printed and bound in China by C&C Offset Printing Co., Ltd

ISBN 978-1-43230-917-6

This book is printed on FSC®-certified paper. Forest Stewardship Council® (FSC®) is an independent, international, non-governmental organization. Its aim is to support environmentally sustainable, socially and economically responsible global forest management.

Follow Kobus on Instagram @kobusbraai, Facebook @kobusbraai, YouTube channel Kobus Braai, www.kobusbraai.fr